How NOT to DATE or MARRY the MENTALLY ILL

ED RIEGER

Fulton Books
Meadville, PA

Published by Fulton Books 2024

ISBN 979-8-88982-469-5 (paperback)
ISBN 979-8-89221-884-9 (hardcover)
ISBN 979-8-88982-470-1 (digital)

Printed in the United States of America

PSYCHOLOGICAL PARADIGM SHIFT MOVEMENT

This paradigm shift will define human communication and decision-making for the twenty-first century. What is a paradigm shift? Consider things around you today that you think are normal and you've grown accustomed to and then tomorrow, some new information or technology is created, and what was normal to you yesterday is not normal today. In history, we have experienced many paradigm shifts. One day, we rode horses for transportation, then we invented automobiles, and they changed transportation forever. One day, we used hard-line telephones, then we invented the iPhone. I remember using carbon paper with manual typewriters, then we invented personal and industrial computers. We used to own other humans, then we didn't. Paradigm shifts usher in new ways of thinking and behaving. That is what the psychological paradigm shift movement is about.

I have been concerned for a long time that we humans are devolving, not evolving. The reason for this de-evolution is that we have never really gotten a grip on the primary cause of all social and human conflicts, mental illness. Psychological disorders have been with us since Cain and Abel or the Sumerian King Gods Enlil and Enki. Mental illness has been part of our societal makeup forever, and until we put concrete actions in place to eliminate it, it always will be.

Mental illness is one of the oldest human diseases we suffer from. It is also the most undiagnosed and untreated disease we have. It is 2023, and the psychiatric community finally acknowledged the massive level of Americans suffering from a mental disorder and decided to create a 988-telephone number for people who are in psychological distress to call for help. We spend trillions of dollars annually and employ millions of people trying to manage the behaviors and actions of the mentally ill. The costs are staggering for such things as the defense budget, facilities for addictions, policing, court systems, facilities for mental illness treatments, psychotropic drugs, imprisonment facilities, child welfare, foster care. I could go on and on. I believe this psychological paradigm shift is the concrete action necessary to get a handle on mental illness in the twenty-first century and beyond.

The psychological paradigm shift has three phases; I have written three books to introduce the reasons we need to shift our thinking and how to do it. These three phases of the psychological paradigm shift were designed for you to use personally, and we will use societally to combat mental illness at its core. I am going to take direct actions personally to bring this paradigm shift to life. With all the fascists activities throughout the world, especially in the United States, we have hit a critical moment. We can no longer count on the goodwill of other citizens, outdated laws, leaders, societal norms, and institutional governance to wish mental illness and the behaviors of the mentally ill away. We must act. This paradigm shift is the beginning of taking control of the actions of the mentally ill, what we experience daily as normal currently, and what we will experience as our daily normal tomorrow.

How Not to Date or Marry the Mentally Ill is the first action I am taking. Nothing will affect you more personally than creating a long-term romantic partnership with another human being. Transparency and knowledge are the key to this paradigm shift. You must know as much as possible about how your potential partner thinks and behaves. I have created twenty-seven categories and 802 questions for you to use while you are dating to help you understand the psychological makeup of your potential partner.

I believe the next two phases of the psychological paradigm shift will be just as impactful to us personally and to our society. Hopefully, it will help us evolve in a more positive direction. I am going to introduce the next two phases soon. I hope you join the movement. Good luck to us all.

Go to www.psychologicalparadigmshift.com for updates of the movement.

INTRODUCTION

Unfortunately for the mentally healthy, the mentally ill do not come with labels tattooed on their foreheads. It would be fantastic if there were a radar system to let you know when you are dealing with someone who has a mental disorder. We just must guess, hope, pray, and assume everything.

The purpose of this book is to help you avoid the mentally ill while you are dating and potentially deciding to marry someone who may have a mental disorder. If I can help you avoid the bad choices that are made every day by the mentally healthy who just do not see the red flags, then this book has helped you. The mentally ill live in constant psychological tornadoes. Make no mistake, they will pull you in and destroy you and the ones you love without giving it a second thought.

I was raised by a single mother who was an alcoholic; she lived in a constant state of chaotic nightmares, and so did I. I am not a psychiatrist or psychologist, and I do not have the same training they've had. What I do have is sixty-three years of direct living experience as someone who grew up in severe mental illness, and I have struggled with the effects my entire life. I have studied many of the technical and diagnostic manuals to help change my thinking and behavior. I constantly monitor my thinking and behavior to strive to be as mentally healthy as possible.

I believe our purpose on this planet is to reach for our full potential as human beings every day. This book is my way of reaching for mine. I hope this knowledge will benefit you. Let's get started.

There are not enough Oscars for the world-class performances being acted out every day by the mentally ill while they are dating and when they marry.

If you have read this far and think "I am smarter than the mentally ill," "I can see them coming a mile away," "I will be ten steps ahead of them," and "I can avoid getting involved no matter what they throw at me," just watch the news, listen to your family and friends, and hear the horror stories that happen every day of the financially destroyed the physically and psychologically abused and even those killed by the mentally ill.

The mentally ill are not stupid or ignorant people; they can be very intelligent, slick, and charismatic individuals. They come from all walks of life, all races, and all ethnic and social groups. Mental illness does not care if you are white, black, Hispanic, Asian, or Martian, or if you are rich, poor, or have a family history dating back to the pharaohs of Egypt. It affects every ethnic and economic group in the world (Mark Banschick, MD, *Psychology Today*, February 6, 2012).

The only difference between the mentally ill and you are that you are willing to educate yourself about how not to be abused by them and they are not interested in learning how not to abuse you. Their only concern is their own selfish needs and desires. You are only a means to an end for them. What you need or want has little meaning to them. Their daily lives are all about chaos.

The National Alliance on Mental Illness has cited that roughly one in five of all Americans suffer from some form of mental disorder in any given year (NAMI, July 23, 2018). If that is a fact, that is over sixty million Americans. With approximately seven billion people on this planet, that is 1.4 billion humans with some kind of mental disorder. That is a lot of people with depression, paranoid psychosis, narcissistic personality disorder, conduct disorder, schizophrenia, and sociopathic disorders. There are so many more disorders to list; I could be here all day. Some mentally ill individuals even have multiple disorders, especially when it comes to personality disorders. You can see this very clearly in paranoid personality disorder, narcissistic personality disorders, and antisocial disorders. It is virtually impossible to keep up with an individual juggling multiple disorders, especially if you add money and power to the mix.

The point is, if you think you don't need to educate yourself about the mentally ill as you are starting to put yourself out there in the dating pool, then you might want to check your own narcissistic issues. When you think of the sixty million Americans with mental disorders and you think of how many people they encounter daily—their children, spouses, siblings, parents, coworkers, priests, rabbis, you get the picture—if they can induce just one person from their inner circle, then the sixty million becomes 120 million. If the 1.4 billion can induce just one person each, that is 2.8 billion. Avoiding them is not an option; knowing what you are dealing with is the only option. That is the purpose of this book.

I will try and show my personal experiences growing up in a mentally ill family and what I have come to understand through time about how mental illness has affected every decision I have made and every relationship I have had and how it has led me to this moment to try and shed some light on how you can use my experiences and knowledge to not date or marry the mentally ill. I am not here to cry about my past or gain any sympathy from anyone. This is how I see things, and I hope it will help you.

Fifty percent of first marriages, 67 percent of second marriages, and 73 percent of third marriages end in divorce. Why is that? Who's to blame? What is the cost emotionally, physically, and financially? I will do everything in this book to make sure you avoid being part of these statistics. Hopefully, after you are exposed to the information I am going to share with you, it will give you the right ammunition to save yourself from the time-wasting, destructive, financially devastating, and life-threatening experience of dating or marrying the mentally ill. I will introduce some technical psychological terms from time to time only to help you understand the depth of the mental disorder you may encounter.

I believe the inducement of mental disorders is the most powerful effect that the mentally ill have. This is the number one tool in their arsenal that all mentally ill individuals depend on to sway, encourage, and manipulate in their quest to make you live in their chaotic tornado. Let me explain what this is. Inducement is when someone with a mental illness transfers their mental illness and the negative effects over to you, either when you are a child and being raised by them or when they have financial, social, political, religious, or physical power and control over you. They are master manipulators—cunning, sly, pathologically dishonest, morally corrupt, and potentially very, very dangerous. As I will show you, by the time you meet them, they have had decades to learn and perfect their skills to persuade.

I have broken the book down into two sections, the first will discuss the timelines of the mentally ills' lives and how, when, and what affects mental illness has on them and possibly you. I will show the two sides of the coin when it comes to mental illness: are they born with a mental disease or have their brains been damaged by some outside influence, or are they taught how to be mentally ill? The second section of the book will be the twenty-seven categories and the eight-hundred-plus questions that I have created to help you navigate your way through this new paradigm shift of dating.

This is the twenty-first century, human communication must evolve, and the key to that communication is going to be education and knowledge. You must educate yourself to the psychological foundation of the person you are trying to create possibly a lifelong bond too. You cannot make dating and marriage decisions based on physical, religious, economic, or social factors any longer. Psychology must become part of our tool belt when dating; we must be able to see past the red flags that people throw at us when dating or potentially marrying. The questions are structured in categories to help you understand the timelines of the person's life. The questions are very tough and possibly extremely sensitive; you will have to put on your detective hat to determine when to ask them and in what context.

This book is a guide to help you see the real person you are trying to date or potentially going to marry and make a permanent commitment to. The questions were designed to entice the information from your potential partner so you can make an informed decision. The book and questions provided will empower you to gain the knowledge necessary from your potential partner to hopefully make the right decision when it comes to dating and potentially marrying them.

CHAPTER 1

Ready or Not, Here I Come— Ages Zero to Eighteen

Where does mental illness come from? Thankfully, we have psychologists and neuroscientists that have helped answer many of these questions. Mental illness is no longer a mystery, hidden away in an institution, attic, or basement, to be shunned and ostracized from society. Mental illness has become mainstreamed into our medicine cabinets, school systems, gun debates, driving license divisions, politics, employment, and overall society. Mental illness is a national and international conversation and concern. In July of 2023, President Biden even proposed activities to address mental illness directly. Mental illness has been with humanity since the beginning of our known history. The kings of Sumer, Enlil and Enki, which the Sumerians are recognized as humanity's first culture, taught all of us how to war, kill, and rape each other. The Bible's Cain and Abel taught us how to murder one another. In his brilliant book, *Madness in Civilization* (Princeton University Press, 2015), Andrew Scull perfectly describes the full history of mental illness from our beginnings to current times.

The main three reasons an individual will become inflicted with a mental disorder is neurological, environmental, and inducement. Let's look at the first two, but I will spend most of the book on the inducement category.

1

If you have ever read a book on neuroscience (e.g., *Neuroscience: Exploring the Brain* by Mark F. Bear PhD, Barry W. Connors PhD, Michael A. Paradiso PhD, Jones, and Bartlett Learning), which is the study of the brain, you will be blown away at how the brain works. It will be the most fascinating book you have ever read and possibly the most complex and difficult. The human brain is the most complex and mysterious organ on our planet. The brain's abilities are stunning and mind-blowingly fascinating. With the invention of electronic magnetic imaging, the brain's long unknown functions have become illuminated. Neuroscientists have been able to crack the code of the brain's functioning ability and are on the verge of tremendous and enlightening abilities to benefit society when it comes to the neurological diseases of the brain. Neuroscientists have begun to understand the chemistry of the brain and functioning to such a degree that they now are creating life-changing medications for such things as depression and schizophrenia. Stunning! Unfortunately, humanity still has thousands of years of the foundations of mental illness woven into our societal norms and behaviors, and no microscope or psychotropic medication can fix that by tomorrow. But having this knowledge will help us educate ourselves further as we strive to understand our fellow humans' behaviors and actions.

The environmental reasons that a person can be afflicted with a mental disorder are extremely varied. You can ingest a chemical like lead that will cause possible damage to the brain's functioning. You could be in a car accident and receive a traumatic brain injury. The environmental reasons are endless and complex. Does poverty play a role because of lack of proper nutrition or no nutrition? Does exposure to violence play a role? As society accepts the reasonings of mental illness from the neurological to induced psychosis and environmental causes, the knowledge will help all of us evolve to a more enlightened society.

When we talk about the many mental disorders that we humans are afflicted with from depression, schizophrenia, to personality disorders, neuroscience and psychologists talk about the percentages of people in society who may be suffering from this illness or that illness. But what is not discussed is the number of people that are currently being exposed to individuals who are suffering from a mental disorder over the thousands of years of exposure that has solidified the fabric of our societal and psychological foundations.

I believe the frank and enlightening discussion about mental illness is the discussion for the twenty-first century; it will determine how we move forward as a society and species. Medical professionals cannot explain the many reasons we humans continue to behave in destructive, abusive, self-defeating, and de-evolving ways. When world leaders are embroiled in murderous combat and have the power to unleash nuclear annihilation, I believe it is the exact time to have harsh conversations about mental illness and the neurological and environmental reasons that are attributable to many mental disorders throughout history and the causes of many societies and human woes today.

Because I believe mental illness is the oldest and most undiagnosed disease in human history, the inducement of one generation to the next is the main culprit when it comes to many of the abuses we inflict on each other. I believe that when it comes to mental illness, the neurological and environmental reasons are dwarfed in comparison to mental illness caused by induced psychosis.

The one thing we humans do not get to choose is our parents and families. Whatever elevator we jump on to get down here doesn't come with the button of choice or the family we get to have. It is like throwing dice, you win some and you lose some. It's a crapshoot.

The question is, does the family you get have mental disorders or not? If they do not, you have a chance at a normal upbringing. The picket fence is your reality, not the fantasy. If your family does have mental disorders, then get ready for the tornado because it is getting ready to flatten your picket fence and to teach you how to flatten every picket fence you dream of building.

When you are dealing with the mentally ill, you must be very critical of them and the red flags they lob over your head. Knowing their family history and background will be the beginning of knowing who they are and what kind of abuse they may inflict on you. I don't care if someone is Jewish, Indian, black, wealthy, poor, Republican, or Democrat. When you are searching for a mentally healthy person to date and marry, you won't either. One of the first things you want to be very aware of with the mentally ill is the lack of information from them.

When they are young, they have no idea as to the chaos they have been born into. For them, everything is perfectly normal, like moving constantly, ongoing money problems, alcoholism, drug addiction, men and women going in and out of their lives, or the idea that being physically and sexually abused is normal for all children and families. They do not understand that you don't have to constantly be perfect or overly religious or afraid of all germs and physical contact.

You can guarantee one thing: they will not like talking about their childhoods, or they give very brief descriptions and then change the subject quickly. Their family history is completely different from yours. They will fabricate family memories to suit the moment, or they may create experiences that are false because they cannot bear the reality they experienced and don't think you can either. You are going to have to become quite the psychological detective to uncover the truth of their real childhood. Whatever disorder their parents have has been drilled into them over the last eighteen years. Knowing as much about their childhood as quickly as possible will be a godsend to you. It will most likely give you the ammunition you need to decide how much further you want to take this relationship or whether to get out as fast as you can.

I believe disorders manifest in two ways: passive and aggressive. I have found that most women will think and act out in passive-aggressive or self-defeating ways, and men will think and act out in aggressive ways. Both will be just as devastating to you by the time they get done dragging you into their chaos.

Because of the psychological inducement by their parents, siblings, and family members in their younger years, their reality seems perfectly normal to them. When you come along and they interact with you, always remember that they have become or are becoming very perceptive of how to read your body language, facial cues, tone, and any sign you can project that helps them gain knowledge of how to sell the package you are looking for. They are chameleonlike, always recreating and reinventing themselves so as not to lose favor. They need you to be induced; without your willingness to let them control the relationship, they have no interest in you.

Once a man or boy understands that he can use his physical abilities, he may stop the charms and become very physical—unless he internally realizes that abusing others is not right. I will talk about men who fit into this category later. Women, I have found, will always use their sexual charms. I believe boys and girls both learn to use their sexual attraction to lure you in at a very early age. It is convincing, powerful, quick, inducing, and extremely effective.

I think the mentally ill learn from firsthand knowledge and experience that sex is a tool and is the quickest way to disarm their prey. They do not have the same barriers as you and are usually a lot more experienced. They may have been having sex since they were very young children and usually with older siblings, parents, other family members, or strangers. They know how to turn on sexual charms and have zero problems with morality. According to a 2017 CDC report, 40 percent of US high school students have had sexual intercourse at least once, 10 percent of students had four or more sexual partners, 30 percent had had sex during the previous three months and of these, 46 percent did not use a condom the last time they had sex, and 14 percent of those surveyed did not use any method of contraception.

The mentally ill will want to become physical immediately. They will always test the waters to see how far you are willing to go. They are not worried about diseases, pregnancy, or any consequences that you think are normal. With the Supremes Court's decision in 2022 to overturn *Roe v. Wade* and the CDC's report of unprotected sex percentages, it can be life altering if there's an unwanted pregnancy. Abortion is not an option in multiple states any longer, and you will be stuck parenting a child long before either person is psychologically, financially, or educationally capable.

One of the biggest signs you will want to be aware of are family secrets—topics or family members that are off-limits. Family secrets are the solar flares of every family. The family members think their secrets are the holy grail of the family, not to be talked about, revealed, or even whispered about. For you, it is the sign that there are some very serious issues being hidden in that family. They struggle with addressing the chaos that they live in. They want to avoid these conversations like the plague. For you, it is the big red flag that has bullet holes all through it.

This is where you must be very careful. The mentally ill will use these family secrets to induce you. They may weep or become depressed over their family issues, but do not be fooled. It is not your fault their family has secrets or problems. Do not let them suck you in with their histrionics. And if you think they will not use their secrets and chaos or tragedies to manipulate you, dream on. Not discussing the issues with you in a transparent manner is another way for them to manipulate you now that you are becoming part of the inner circle, keeping the secret with them. Either way, you are being manipulated.

Remember, you are not dealing with families who love one another, who are supportive of one another, or who live honestly with each other. You are dealing with families who have extremely ugly histories of abandoning their own children, raping their children, or physically and mentally abusing them. Parents who may have serious alcohol and drug usage problems—current and past. Siblings that may be sexually and physically and psychologically abusing one another. Mentally ill families have devastatingly horrific family secrets. If you choose to get personally and romantically involved with someone who has a mentally ill parent or mentally ill siblings, you will have to live with whatever secrets they are all hiding together.

The question will be, how much do you want to know about them? Their history and family issues? Is the relationship you are trying to create worth caring about the kind of childhood or family they come from? Is the bond you feel with them strong enough for you to continue trying to build a relationship with them, or do you cut and run to save yourself the future devastations that await you?

Of course, as we all must do, you must look at your own family and their issues and be as brutally honest as you can about them. Do you have a family history or secrets that can be viewed as abusive?

Can you relate to the person you are trying to create a relationship with, or is your family healthy based on mentally healthy behavior from your parents and other family members? If you cannot relate in any way, should you not even try to establish a relationship with anyone with a mentally ill family history and background?

In the next chapter, I am going to show you why in the long term, the decision you are facing on whether to create a relationship with a mentally ill person is not recommended. For them and anyone involved with them, life does not get better as they get older, just worse.

CHAPTER 2

Shedding the Parental Skin— Ages Eighteen to Thirty

Imagine you are eighteen years old and you have grown up in a category five storm of chaos and now you are considered an adult, where do you go from here? Of course, that is if you have avoided getting pregnant or being put in prison. I believe as children of the mentally ill age out, it is the most critical time for them.

Remember the causes of mental illness are very few: you are either born with a neurological disorder or some outside influence like lead has caused damage to your brain, you have a traumatic brain injury, or you were born to mentally ill parents and they have trained you how to be mentally ill like them. Depending on many factors, the damage done may be even more dramatic; if you were born into poverty, the lack of knowledge and financial resources for therapy and treatment means that your psychological or neurological disorders have never been diagnosed or treated and possibly healed or at least manageable. Psychological-psychiatric treatment is expensive; the average hourly rate is between $90 and $500 per hour. I know firsthand when you grow up in poverty and psychological damage is done to you, you never receive any counseling or support. It is like your arm is broken and no cast is put on it and you live your life with that broken and damaged arm. Always remember, that if the parents are the abusers of the child, then they have no incentive to get therapy for their child or do they even care to. For that parent, abusing their child is as normal as breathing.

Now comes a very tough time for the mentally ill who are aging out of their family home, and for you, this transitioning time between their childhood and adulthood may be the difference between life and death. I don't mean a sudden violent death although that could be the case. I mean a possible slow decade after decade mental and physical death of your mind and soul if you get romantically involved with a mentally ill person.

When you grow up in a mentally ill family, you are literally unaware that anyone in your family suffers from a mental disorder. You have no clue that having parents that are alcoholics or drug addicts is abnormal or that relatives, parents, siblings, or strangers having sex with you is abnormal. If you do not have food or are homeless, you assume every child grows up like you. That is the foundation of your normalcy.

When you are mentally ill, there are a few paths that you can take. In path one, you will stay mentally ill and go about your merry way, creating as much chaos as possible. This mentally ill person is what I call a chaos chaser. In path two, the fog of mental illness will begin to lift, and the inducement of mental illness will begin to wash away. This mentally ill person is what I call a fog lifter.

Of course, if you are thinking I would rather be involved with the fog lifter and not the chaos chaser, not so fast. Let's look at both and make sure who and what we are dealing with.

Chaos Chasers

The mentally ill who can never change their thinking or behavior are chaos chasers, and you want to avoid them at all costs. Either their brain has a serious disease, they have had some traumatic damage of the brain, or their inducement was so severe they can never come out of the chaos they grew up in.

Am I saying you should never try and create a romantic relationship with them ever? Yes, that is exactly what I am saying. Does this mean chaos chasers cannot change? No, I think they can, but when? What kind of life event would it take for them to change? How dramatic would that life-altering paradigm shift have to be? Are you willing to take the gamble of your life with them? Can you see them ever looking inside themselves deep enough to seek professional help or to self-analyze their behavior and thinking? Is it possible? In my sixty-three years on this planet, I have never seen any of the chaos chasers I know change, unfortunately, for everyone who has had to be abused by them.

They will most likely have serious legal problems; they are always doing something unlawful. They are into drugs, alcohol, and any behavior that is antisocial. They usually have children in their teens, usually with different people. They struggle to keep consistent employment. Let me just say here that I have seen some chaos chasers that can keep consistent employment with the same employer their entire adult lives with no problems at their worksite, but when it comes to their home life, that is a whole other picture—multiple divorces, child molestation, spousal abuse, drug usage, alcohol abuse, incarceration, or multiple incarcerations. Their finances may always be a disaster. They will not or cannot educate themselves to try and evolve past their past or current situation.

The chaos chaser is obvious; avoiding them should not be a question. Knowing their family's background and their current mental status is still critical if they should somehow try and put on a Hollywood performance for you. Remember, they are not hiding in their basement sitting in the dark. They are free to interact with anyone they want in society, and that means potentially dating you.

According to the FBI, romance scams account for over $200 million in damages to victims every year. And that is what victims are willing to report.

Domestic violence is rampant in America, with most states having to create domestic sheltering and police having to learn special questioning methods when called to a domestic disturbance.

According to the CDC, over 30 percent of women experience violent sexual assault every year. The lifetime cost of these assaults to the victims is $122,461 through lost wages and medical expenses. And 33 percent of women rape victims and 25 percent of male victims experience their first sexual assault between the ages of eleven and seventeen.

Every night on the six o'clock news, we hear one story after another of chaos chasers committing every kind of violent act imaginable, from rape to home invasions, robberies, embezzlement, and murder. I could give you one statistic after another, from alcohol and drug treatment facilities to the amount of child abuse from family members. I think you are getting the picture.

Chaos chasers are the most dangerous of the mentally ill to our society and to you if you get romantically involved with them. Knowledge will be the only weapon you have against them. Knowing as much about their childhood and teen years will make the biggest difference for you.

Fog Lifters

Now this is where things get tricky. Between the ages of eighteen and thirty, it is a critical time for fog lifters. They are now most likely on their own financially and psychologically. They have probably found a way to break away from their families; even though they may not know it consciously, they have. They may have joined the military, moved in with high school friends, or enrolled in school. They are trying desperately to distance themselves from their families and the chaos they grew up in, again, not knowing that is what they are doing. Their subconscious is trying to create a barrier of distance to start the separation that is going to take place over the next decade.

They are beginning to realize, through interactions with others, how different they really are. When they talk with associates and hear about their families and the kind of social interactions, educational achievements, and positive personal relationships they have, it can be mind-boggling. These are life events and connections with other family members and other people that they have no clue about. Remember, they most likely grew up isolated socially and physically and abused sexually, mentally, and physically. If their parents had alcohol or substance addictions, they grew up neglected physically, emotionally, financially, and socially.

Depending on the seriousness of the traumas that they experienced in their childhood, many of them will suffer from what is titled as "complex PTSD." The abuse they experienced has now entrenched itself in the subconscious of their minds. As they age, they will slowly begin to unravel the very complicated psychological damage done to them. Their memories are nonexistent, scattered, jumbled, foggy, and squirreled away in many corners. The memories will come back in flashes and pieces according to their ability to comprehend and accept them. Some memories are as black as the universe, never to be explored again. Other memories will come back as clear as day even if it is decades later. If they have complex PTSD, they will always have it; their burden will be how to manage it and survive through it.

Many of the people I have given this book to who I know have suffered very traumatic childhoods all have the same reaction. First they read a few pages, cry, then put the book down. They tell me that they just can't go there, and we never talk about it again.

When a fog lifter is listening to you talk about positive life events with your loved ones, they may act like they are listening and like they are understanding and concerned. What they are really doing is trying to think of an escape route. How can they change the subject and misdirect you so you don't ask them anything about them or their background? At younger ages, fog lifters are developing skills to avoid discussions about themselves that can create minefields. When you ask some of the questions I am going to give you, become very aware of how they answer and especially how they avoid them. I do not believe most fog lifters are trying to deceive you or to hurt you; they are trying to protect themselves, not knowing that it isn't going to help them anyway to try and manipulate the relationship.

As they begin to break away from the mental inducement of their parents, they probably will not have any financial or emotional support from the family in any substantial means. You can see this manifest itself in the educational or business world very clearly. Fog lifters who are smart will commit themselves 100 percent to achieving some sort of educational or financial success. Their psychological objective will be to excel at their chosen path no matter how ill-prepared, uneducated, or unrealistic it may be. Now if they can figure out how to get an influential education, this can go a long way in the kind of careers they can follow and the kinds of life paths they can take.

Make no mistake, just because they can get a strong education, even in Ivy League schools, it doesn't mean they are not mentally ill and do not have the ability to destroy you if you become romantically involved. The number of women raped on college campuses is 26.4 percent; for men, it is 6.8 percent, according to rainn.org. I think if any fog lifter does commit any violent act against another person, then they have just moved into the chaos chaser category and probably will never come out of their fog.

Fog lifters will always be working, even on holidays and vacations. I once worked for seven years without a vacation and hardly a day off. Even to this day, I can work for many years without substantial time off.

Many fog lifters, currently, are probably drinking heavily or doing drugs to suppress their emotional pain and hide their past from themselves. They may have difficulties holding down jobs. Their finances are messy, their credit is bad, and they will probably file for bankruptcy.

Now unlike a chaos chaser, fog lifters do not want or cannot think of having children. Their subconscious knows that if they have children, they are most likely going to repeat the mentally ill behavior of their parents. This is a major sign of a fog lifter.

Unfortunately for you and the fog lifter, stopping yourselves from having children is virtually impossible. Lack of control, social demands, religious beliefs, and, yes, family pressures can force fog lifters into giving in and being weak. This will make things very difficult for you and them in their struggle to move beyond their childhood paradigms. That is why I think so many people divorce not once but multiple times.

Fog lifters are making mistakes between ages eighteen and thirty that result in children they really should not have had. I see it all the time in young families. The young women are left with children with no men around to support them emotionally, financially, or physically. The men have no contact with the children because they just don't want to or because they are incarcerated or because of a thousand other reasons. Either way, the cycle of mental illness repeats. The women are to blame also; they cannot see their own mental illness, and they cannot see the men's. The victims here are the children and the continued regurgitation of disorders.

This is extremely critical. You must avoid having children with fog lifters at all costs. You will tie yourself to them for the rest of your life. You will have to deal with the insanity of the decisions and mistakes they make as they transform to be as mentally healthy as possible if they ever do. You will have to associate with their family and friends if they still interact with them for a very long time, maybe forever.

This is the most dangerous part: your children may be involved with the same parents, siblings, and other relatives that the fog lifter grew up with. Your future children may grow up receiving the same kinds of abuse that your fog lifter lived with. Once you have the child, it is too late to turn the train around. What if you divorce and the fog lifter starts dating someone or marries them and they have the same background as the fog lifter or worse? Now your child is spending time with this person and possibly their parents and siblings and other family members. That is why becoming romantically involved with a fog lifter and imagining that you can have children with them is insane.

If you meet a fog lifter who has chosen not to have children at all or at some later date, do not assume you are dealing with someone who will one day wake up and be perfectly normal. At no time will a fog lifter or chaos chaser ever be as normal as you have been raised. When fog lifters consider having children and realistically accept the history of their childhood, they know they cannot bring a child into their lives. And if you want to have children before you are thirty or forty, becoming involved with a fog lifter is very unrealistic. I have noticed over the years that many of the young adults I know are choosing not to have children even in their forties, and many of them are not marrying at all. According to the Census Bureau, the median age for first marriages is over thirty. According to the World Bank, the birth rate for the United States in 1.64 per women and declining. It is even worst in Europe and China.

Just because fog lifters do not want to have children does not mean they are not chaos bombs waiting to go off. They will make some really devastating mistakes, socially, personally, and financially. They are subconsciously trying to change their familial, social, educational, and financial paradigms. They may be willing to take serious financial risks to create financial independence. Remember, they have started looking at the reality of their families, knowing consciously or subconsciously that they cannot count on their families. Financial independence will give them the control and power they know they must have. Mentally ill families have the weakest support systems of all families. They will leave each other for dead when it comes to finances or emotional needs. My experience is they do not leave wills, trusts, life insurance, or any kind of savings. If they do, it is a chaotic mess where family members try to steal everything from one another when parents, grandparents, or siblings pass away.

Mentally ill parents are absorbed in their own chaos storms and cannot be focused on their children's needs. Fog lifters know this subconsciously, and you will see their behaviors reflect it, especially when it comes to finances. Most likely, the fog lifter will fail at the financial endeavor they undertake between eighteen and thirty because they are still caught in the mental tornado of the chaos of their childhood. Unfortunately for you, if you have spent years of your life with them, you will be destroyed also.

Let me explain this very clearly: fog lifters will most likely owe large amounts of money to creditors. They will owe the IRS back taxes, penalties, and interest. The IRS will demand payment, and fog lifters will not have the money. Their family cannot or will not help them. The IRS will garnish their wages for years until every cent is repaid. Their creditors will demand payment, fog lifters will have to file for bankruptcy, and it will destroy their credit for years. They will most likely face homelessness because they are deadass broke. Or if they have somehow made a financial success of themselves in some endeavor like sports, they will behave and act out in some fashion that will jeopardize the financial successes they have experienced.

For you, this would be a real joyride of mental, financial, and emotional stress that is unimaginable. Here you are tied to this financial nuclear bomb, the stress of facing living in the streets, and years of financial and emotional stress and devastation would destroy you, emotionally, physically, financially, and psychologically.

This would take place over a very long time, depending on how long it takes to dig yourself out of this financial mess. What if by this time you have children? I have seen families living in tents for extended periods while they dug themselves out of the chaos. It is a nightmare for the children and everyone involved.

Fog lifters are very dangerous people to be in a relationship with, especially between eighteen and thirty, and can still be just as dangerous in their forties and fifties. If they have the mental awareness that their thinking and behavior is flawed, hopefully they will seek psychiatric help to try and reconcile the negative impact of their childhood and the disastrous early adult years. That is if somehow they have medical insurance or the financial means to afford therapy. Most likely, they have made so many mistakes by this time in their jobs or businesses, and these may be in jeopardy or destroyed. Or they have so many children to pay for that it may be impossible to afford therapy. They may be lost forever. Now if they can stand still and think clearly, their subconscious will drive them to try to understand why they make such disastrous decisions.

For fog lifters, there is a sliver of hope in the public library. They will figure out that the local library is free and that they carry psychology books. They can study the DSM (*Diagnostic and Statistical Manual of Mental Disorders*) and other psychology manuals to educate themselves and to analyze their thinking and behavior. It will be long and difficult. They will have to devote all their energy and free time to studying and self-reflection. Most likely, it will take many years if they have any hope of coming out of the fog of their mental illness.

They will have to do all this while trying to build some kind of financial stability in their employment. Remember, they will be self-analyzing with no support from their family in any way, shape, or form. It will be very isolating and lonely, and it will take every ounce of mental strength and discipline they can muster to stay focused and not make life-altering mistakes while they attempt to heal.

What does that mean for you? It means that if by any way possible you have survived with a fog lifter by this point, it is probably the end of the road for you and the relationship you thought you had. The fog lifter is going to have to use every spare moment to study or reflect on their past; it is going to be very difficult for them to face the ugly reality of their lives up to this moment. They will not have a second to spare to be concerned with your needs. If you have no problem being neglected and spending time by yourself, then you are probably a fog lifter yourself, and we'll discuss later what that means to relationships between fog lifters.

We have looked at the childhoods of the mentally ill, and we have looked at their lives as they age between eighteen and thirty. I hope I am helping you see that the years between eighteen and thirty are extremely critical in the psychological and financial transition taking place in the lives of the mentally ill.

Remember, this is a deep, entrenched, rock-solid mentally damaged conditioning that took hold in the chaos chaser and fog lifters for decades; it is their foundation of thinking. Most mentally ill individuals will never come out of the darkness. I believe only fog lifters have a chance of changing their paradigms. It will not be easy, and they will always have to analyze their actions and thoughts as they age and interact with others. It will be a lifelong illness that cannot be cured but can be managed.

Sex with the Mentally Ill

I wanted to make sure I covered this topic all by itself because I believe it is one of the major causes of broken relationships and divorces when it comes to the mentally ill. Like all relationships, at first, everything is exciting, romantic, and pleasurable. As you begin the sexual activities in your relationship, everything is fantastic or not, but most of the time, you are very satisfied with your sexual activities with each other. You are still in the honeymoon stage, and everything is just fine. As time goes on and this may be years, not

days or weeks, your sexual relationship begins to change. It is grad-
ual, slow-moving, and almost unnoticeable until years later. As the
walls have come down and you learn more facts from your significant
other or spouse, you may learn about the devastating sexual history
of their childhood. You learn that parents, siblings, and other family
members were raping them throughout their childhood and teenage
years. Or they were raped by a stranger or strangers. If you did not
have this happen to you as a child, I do not know how you would
cope with this knowledge of your partner. If it had happened to you
also, you understand their history and don't think twice about it.
But as your spouse or significant other feels safer with you, their
true sexual desires and behaviors may begin to emerge. Things in the
bedroom begin to change. Sexual activities that you used to enjoy
together may become more infrequent or nonexistent. The confu-
sion of these behaviors and activities will go unspoken, chalked up to
fatigue, or a thousand other excuses that become acceptable. The joy
and passion of your relationship begins to fade until time has driven
a wedge through it, and it may not be fixable.

You try to understand and accept where the relationship has
landed, but it is difficult to continue with your partner. As people
mature and become more entrenched in their sexual activities, they
are not willing to participate in certain activities because of the damage done to them as children; it becomes obvious that your relationship with them cannot continue on this path. This is where I believe
relationships are in jeopardy of ending in separation or divorce.

Another situation might arise. Your partner may have a change
in their sexual desires because they were introduced to sexual situa-
tions very early in life, and they may be drawn to sexual activities that
you just can't handle, such as bondage, threesomes, foursomes, bisex-
uality, homosexuality, outdoor sex, and many other forms of expres-
sions of sexual activities. If you find this appalling and unacceptable,
then the relationship could be over. Your partner might come to realize things about themselves in this sexual journey that will alter your
relationship forever unless you come to enjoy the same things.

When we are dating and beginning to get to know each other, we
avoid talking about certain taboo subjects like sexual desires because

we are afraid of scaring each other off. Because we don't communicate about what we like and don't like to do sexually, it can become the make-or-break topic in our relationships. I've included this topic because I have lived through these issues in my relationships, and it was one of the big reasons for separation or a change in our sexual activities.

When you bring other activities or beliefs into the mix, like religious beliefs or social standings, your partners changing sexual desires and activities might be completely unacceptable. Because most religions have no flexibility to their foundational beliefs on sexual behaviors, then your relationship may be over no matter if you're the religious one or the one who has adopted different sexual desires and activities.

Understanding that a big part of sexual traumas will alter the way a child or individual will relate to sex, sexual desires, and sexual activities, if you attempt to date or marry someone with sexual traumas in their past, you must understand that the sexual relationship you believe you might have with them might not turn out the way that you thought it would. You might have to adjust your thinking and experiment with them, accept the limitations of their sexual activities, or say to yourself, I can't or won't even begin a relationship with someone with sexual traumas in their past. I believe this topic in a relationship is critically important.

When you are young and just learning about your sexual desires and the kinds of sexual activities you like to participate in with a partner, you will probably make mistakes, but that's alright, it's part of life. Knowing as much about your sexual desires and the sexual activities you enjoy and don't enjoy will go a long way in the success of your relationships, especially when trying to date or marry the mentally ill.

CHAPTER 3

Ages Thirty to Forty (Prime Time)

This time frame can be very important for the mentally ill. Unfortunately for the chaos chasers between thirty and forty who never analyzed their childhood or their own mental illness and who are repeating the thoughts and behaviors of their parents, siblings, and relatives, they will be repeating the cycle of alcohol, drugs, raping their children, breaking laws, and causing as much chaos as possible for everyone in their orbit. When they get to the thirty-to-forty timeline, they are in full swing, behaving how they were taught by their parents and families, with their own psychotic twists. Of course, they have had the right to have their children and begin the cycle all over again. If you can avoid chaos chasers between eighteen and forty or anytime during your life, thank the stars and everything you find holy.

Now what about the fog lifters? Where are they between thirty and forty? If, unfortunately, they have had children, they have most likely been divorced once or twice by now or they have had multiple unsuccessful relationships. Most likely, they have not repeated some of the more devastating abuses on their children. They most likely have succumbed to alcoholism, drug addiction, or the dozens of other addictions possible while their subconscious has struggled with their childhood demons.

They probably have had financial troubles. They have had to move multiple times for various reasons. The financial cost of divorcing was devastating unless somehow their spouse was independently wealthy. Their employment has been sketchy; they have probably had many jobs and lost them for various reasons.

If you are thinking of dating a fog lifter with a history of children and exes, you will be dating their children and exes also. Who knows what kind of nightmares you may be walking into? Remember, if the fog lifter dated or married someone before you, that person is most likely mentally ill also. In fact, you can pretty much guarantee it. You have no idea as to the baggage that will come with these exes; you can guarantee it will be years of chaos, especially if they have children together. Then you are tied to the hip with them for the rest of your life.

The fog lifter may have begun therapy or self-analyzation, but they have a long way to go before they see and accept their past. Reconciling their past and accepting their current mental illness will be monumental. In all the chaos, where do you fit in? Do you want to get involved in a relationship that has so many entanglements? Do you know how damaged the exes are? What kind of mental illnesses do the children have? Dealing with the mental issues of the fog lifter is going to be impossible. Can you imagine trying to deal with the mental illnesses of the ex-spouses, children, in-laws on both sides of the entire gaggle of exes, siblings, and other family members? Holy shit!

Like I said before, if you want to jump into the pit of hell during a nuclear storm, go for it. Now if you do, I recommend that you start going to therapy or self-analyze yourself.

I think fog lifters who have had children and are currently raising them are completely off-limits as a dating pool. They may one day evolve to a place of clarity, but they will still have the other chaos bombs in their lives; the future chaos bombs, the children, will age and add to the stress. It's your choice. Walk lightly.

Now as for fog lifters who have decided not to have children or to wait until thirty or forty, I see them as the same. Fog lifters who have begun the process of working through their psychological illnesses through therapy or self-education between eighteen and thirty are on their way to evolving and trying to reach their full potential.

They have fully accepted the devastating reality of their childhood and are doing everything in their power to recreate their realities.

There are no mysteries about who they are and where they came from. They accept the ugliness of their past and the fact that some of their family members will never accept their mental illness and try and change themselves. They know that because of their family's illnesses, they cannot even discuss the past with them and try to accomplish any healing efforts with parents and other family members.

This affects all communications with their families. They most likely have no interaction with their families; there are no holidays, birthdays, or social functions. If they do participate, they usually are not communicating with family except superficially. They want to avoid discussing the unpleasant secrets that exist between them. This is very depressing for the fog lifters because there is nothing they can do about their family's histories.

Some fog lifters know that they cannot ever have children; they can never ever repeat this cycle of insanity. They are choosing to stop the cycle of illness, at least for themselves. They also know they can never count on any of their parents or siblings to help raise their children. They can never expose their children to the mental illness they grew up with. They see the future of their child's life, and the child will never have anything to do with their side of the family. The entire history of their family will have to be erased if they decide to have children. They know that having that child will begin the cycle of secrets, and if they were to allow their child to interact with their family, all the abuse comes with it.

For fog lifters, this can be a very difficult life-altering decision, socially, economically, and personally. We live in a society that almost demands that you have one to twenty kids; there are television shows about the social acceptance of having as many children as possible. Socially, fog lifters are constantly being asked if they have children, and if they don't, why not? This is impossible for fog lifters. Do they tell the truth and explain their family history, or do they come up with a socially acceptable reason to avoid the whole topic? They always avoid the topic because society and the mentally healthy do not want to or cannot hear the truth. Financially, it is difficult because most business associates, clients, bosses, and coworkers want to know why you don't have children, so some fabricated half fact is better. Someday, society may come to accept that one of the truest forms of eliminating mental illness will be to allow fog lifters to have social and economic acceptance for not having children.

When you realize that you cannot or will not have children, the dating pool becomes very limited. Try explaining to a future date that you will never have children. How do you think that will go over? Dating or marrying a fog lifter who has chosen not to have children, either consciously or subconsciously, is a very big deal. You must accept a life of potential social isolation from family and friends. A fog lifter's friends pool is very limited due to years of struggling with their own mental issues and trying to heal from them. Fog lifters can live very lonely lives; if you want to become romantically involved with them, you should be prepared for that kind of existence.

If a fog lifter does decide to have children, they most likely have achieved some kind of financial success, knowing they will have to pay for all the support that will not be available through family. Or the spouse they have chosen might have a mentally healthy family with a lot of support.

There are some major pitfalls that fog lifters do not think of if they decide to have children. What if they die suddenly? Who takes the children? If somehow they had the child with someone whose family is mentally healthy, no problem. What if they have a spouse who is a fog lifter and there aren't any family members to leave the children with? Big problem! So should fog lifters ever have children? Tough call.

CHAPTER 4

After Forty, the Reality Sets In

Chaos chasers are still caught in the tornado. They have most likely had children and induced them in their mentally ill thinking. The cycle gets repeated, with nothing stopping it. They might even be becoming grandparents at this time. Of course, they will have the power to influence a whole new generation. They are very likely on their second, third, or even fourth marriages. They will have children and possibly multiple stepchildren. Who knows how many lives they have touched with their abuses. Some of them may even begin whole new families with younger people. Guaranteeing the cycle of mental illness is perpetuated for decades to come. They can even have children while they are still in prison or if they have a quick break between crimes. Nothing is stopping this nightmare from continuing. No court can stop it, no laws can stop it, no politician can stop it, no religious organization can stop it. The mentally ill, having the unchecked and unregulated right to procreate, is the reason why our societies struggle so desperately with the many abuses of the mentally ill. As neuroscientists and psychiatric professionals learn more and provide more facts, I believe mental illness will be one of the top issues of the twenty-first century.

Fog lifters have a chance of living a full life of the potential they can reach. The reason is they have gotten help in therapy, or they have self-diagnosed their problems, educated themselves, and accepted their reality about themselves and their family's history. Fog lifters can find some peace with their lives. Fog lifters are probably better off trying to date and marry another fog lifter; they can understand their issues better and will most likely have the greatest chance of success.

Make no mistake, if you think you can reverse the history of a fog lifter by dating or marrying them, think again. As fog lifters age, their isolation becomes more profound. Their families do not ever get better; there is no hope in a fog lifter's life that they will ever resemble anything close to normal. The mental illness they grew up in is part of their soul; you can't date it out, you can't marry it out, and you can't change a damn thing about it. Fog lifters know that this is their story and that they will most likely die alone, with no family around them, unless they get very lucky and marry another fog lifter who has somehow evolved past their mentally ill childhood.

Fog lifters may go on in life to accomplish some very interesting things. Because I have no children, I can focus on ideas and projects for decades, like write a book or start a charity. You never know what a fog lifter may use from their life experiences and what they will achieve and what positive effect they may have on society.

As the mentally ill age, the years of broken relationships, failed marriages, and regrets catch up with them, I see that they have given up completely on trying to find love. They accept their fate of living alone, not being entangled in anyone else's dramas. They're exhausted from the efforts of trying to understand the behaviors and actions of potential romantic partners and have reconciled themselves to a single life. Maybe that's why pet ownership has exploded over the years. The clock never goes backward, and once you have used up your time, that's the end. If you are young and reading this book, you have the advantage of time; don't waste it. Educate yourself so you will never regret the clock moving forward.

CHAPTER 5

Conclusion

Today, the mentally ill are free to have children. There are no laws, no social programs, no religious groups, and no educational institutions trying to stop it. No politician is discussing the problem or trying to rectify it with any legislation. The mentally ill are free to create havoc in their own families and on society. We have no structure or system in place to reverse this trend. It is the twenty-first century; we have created spaceships and are eyeing Mars, but no one is doing anything to stop the mentally ill from giving birth and to reverse the cycle of mental illness.

America should create a standard class, like math or science, for psychological education. I believe it is the only solution to reversing the damage of mental illness, especially induced psychosis. We must educate our young people as to what disorders they have been born into. The problem is so large that only mass education is the solution. I do believe, if we start now, it will take decades to remove induced psychosis from America's psychological landscape. How else will we eliminate all the actions of the mentally ill, like rape, xenophobia, child abuse, spouse abuse, embezzlement, romance scams, credit card theft, drug rehab facilities, alcohol rehab facilities, sex rehab facilities, voter suppression, racism, incarcerations, and the endless other actions that the mentally ill perpetuate on society?

In America, we spend trillions of dollars on the mentally ill, on punishment, treatments, and security measures to protect ourselves from them. We all spend so much energy, time, and resources trying to manage the mentally ill; it just strains the soul of our nation. Education and knowledge are the only tools to combat this illness. We must implement immediately psychological education; our nation and the world cannot afford to waste any more time not to. We must empower our youth to evolve past the mental illness they were born into. We must give them a chance to remove the fog of mental illness before they cross over and become the abusers that their parents are. We must give them a chance to heal themselves earlier in life. They must be given a chance at a full and happy existence on this planet. We cannot abandon them and leave their education and healing up to their own efforts. We must accept mental illness for what it is, how much damage it does and has done, and what responsibilities we have as a society to change this paradigm.

I have tried to educate you on who you are dealing with when you want to date or marry the mentally ill. I am a fog lifter, and I spoke about my life and the effects of mental illness as I see it when someone is trying to date or marry us. Mental illness is what you are born with or what you are born into. It doesn't mean you have to date it or marry it.

I will leave you with a positive note. Can the mentally ill find love? I believe they can. I am a fog lifter, and so is my wife. After many failed relationships and years of soul-searching and self-analyzation, we accepted our issues and spent time correcting them before we were willing to reach out for love and joy. We were fortunate to find each other and are ready to celebrate our twenty-fifth anniversary this year. I believe love is part of us reaching for our full potential as human beings. I wish you the best in your quest to find the joys of love. Good luck!

How Not to Date or Marry
the Mentally Ill

---

802 Dating Questions

INTRODUCTION

The goal of these questions is to assist you in being able to decipher the thinking and actions of the person you are dating and potentially going to marry. Since mental illness is usually a lifelong infliction, and I do not know if you are sixteen years old or sixty-five, I have tried to design the questions, so it spans a lifetime. As people become older, their life events become more complex and entangled with long-term relationships, family members, and children. The questions expose the potential dangers that someone with a mental illness poses to you; you must become quite the psychological detective. You will always try to figure out if the person you are dating or planning to marry is mentally ill because of a birth defect of the mechanisms of the brain or have they been exposed to some toxic substance, like lead, or were they induced by their primary caretaker-parent-parents. That is why these questions are so important to you and them.

Hopefully, these questions will protect you and save you from making a terrible life-altering choice no matter what age you are at.

I believe the questions will empower you with the knowledge and tools you will need to see the red flags when thrown in front of you. I structured the questions to give you a foundation for communicating with your potential partner in a very direct and transparent manner, and they should help you expose the exact details you will need to make your assessment.

Some questions are very delicate, and depending on the subject, you may wait to ask them for your in-person dates.

I have broken everything down into twenty-seven categories and then the questions after. I think this will help you keep yourself organized and on track as you begin the questioning phase of your communications.

If you have read *How Not to Date or Marry the Mentally Ill*, these questions will make perfect sense to you and why I designed them the way I did. If the person you are engaging a dating conversation with has not read the book, they may be at a serious disadvantage. To ensure you make the most of your dating experience with them and because you do not want to waste your time, you may recommend they read the book before you start to seriously date them.

Be prepared when you recommend the book and ask these tough questions. The reactions may not be what you expect. These questions may trigger memories from their past they wanted to bury in a dark corner of their minds, or because of the severe trauma they experienced, they may simply not remember events and have blocked entire memories out. Because of their family dynamics, they may have never talked about many of the topics these questions will address with another human being ever! No matter what age they are.

The questions will make a world of difference if you are communicating with a fog lifter or a chaos chaser. I think a fog lifter will be open and ready to take part with this kind of critical honesty to create a substantial dialogue and relationship with you. A chaos chaser might shut down completely and walk away. They cannot address or acknowledge the abuses they have experienced or the abuses they have perpetrated on others in their lifetime. This will give you the opportunity to just walk away from them and save yourself the potential damage they may cause to you.

I designed these questions as a filtering tool. They may help you see quickly who you are dealing with. Listening carefully to the answers people give you will be the key to your ability to decode the secrets they may be hiding.

The questions can show you if you are communicating with someone who has been extremely fortunate to have lived a life free of mental illness and have come from a mentally healthy family or if they have unfortunately come from a world of abuse and neglect and if in their lives they have experienced an extremely traumatic event that has altered their psychological state of mind.

The questions can help you determine how severe the damage has been to your potential dating-marriage partner. Has the damage been mild, severe, or extremely severe? And how have they grown past the damage, or have they ignored it and tried everything in their power to forget about it and avoid it?

The question will be, can you live with the damage to them and accept their issues or not? Of course, you may have to look in the mirror and answer those questions for yourself as well.

Let's begin.

FAMILY HISTORY

The history of their family dynamics may be the biggest red flag for you. Who are their families, and what are they all about? The history of their family will be abuse, neglect, sexual assault, abandonment, and chaos. What you will see very clearly is disconnection from one another.

1. Did you grow up in a two-parent family or single-parent family?
2. How many siblings do you have? Any stepsiblings, how many?
3. Did your parents live in the same house as you grew up in or did they move a lot?
4. Did you know your grandparents, aunts, uncles, cousins?
5. Is your family close?
6. Does your family have reunions?
7. When is the last time you had a reunion?
8. How many people showed up?
9. Do you socialize currently with your parents?
10. When was the last time you did?
11. What did you do?
12. Do you socialize with your siblings?
13. When is the last time you did?
14. What did you do together?
15. Have you ever been excluded from a family social activity?
16. Why?
17. Has the situation ever been resolved with your family?

18. Are you still excluded from family social activities?
19. Have you ever excluded a family member from a family or social event?
20. Why?
21. How many times have your parents been divorced?
22. How many stepbrothers and sisters do you have?
23. How many stepparents do you have?
24. Do you ever socialize with them?
25. When was the last time you socialized with them?
26. What kinds of things do you do with them?
27. At what age were your parents when they had their first child?
28. Were they married or unmarried?
29. Have your parents had children without being married to anyone?
30. Do you have any family memorabilia, like photos?
31. What is your favorite picture?
32. Did your family ever or do they ever take professional family photos of everyone?
33. Does your family do genealogy?
34. Do they share the genealogy with each other?
35. What's your favorite piece of history of your family?
36. Is anyone in your family left out of the genealogy information?
37. Why isn't this information shared with them?
38. Do you participate in collecting the genealogy information?
39. Why not?

ABUSE

Abuse is the number one trauma that many of the mentally ill face very early in life. The abuse they experience is ugly, painful, dehumanizing, long-lasting, and may alter the way the functioning of their brains work. Once a child has been traumatized, who knows what splintering takes place in their souls.

1. Have you ever been physically beaten as a child?
2. Were you beaten by a parent, sibling, grandparent, or other family members, or non-family members?
3. Was there any instrument used to beat you?
4. How often were you beaten?
5. Did you require hospitalization?
6. Did anyone in your family ever verbally abuse you?
7. How often?
8. Were you sexually abused?
9. Was the abuse from a family member or non-family individual?
10. Was it your father, mother, sibling?
11. How often did they abuse you?
12. How many years did the abuse last?
13. Did the family members ever receive treatment for their behavior?
14. Was the abuse ever reported to any law enforcement official, clergy, or educational resource?
15. Did anyone ever get you treatment for the abuse?

16. Do you continue to have a relationship with the person that abused you?
17. How do you socialize with them?
18. How often do you socialize with them?
19. Are you ever alone with them currently?
20. Have you had sex with them recently?
21. When was the last time you had sex with them?
22. If you have children, do you allow the children to be around your abuser?
23. Do you let your children socialize with them?
24. How often?
25. Are your children ever alone with your abuser?
26. Do you know if your abuser abused any of your other siblings?
27. Do your siblings ever socialize with the abuser?
28. What does your siblings do with the abuser socially?
29. Do you and your sibling ever talk about the abuse you received from the abuser?
30. If the abuse did not come from your parents, have you ever spoken to your parents about the abuse?
31. Did any of your siblings receive the same abuse?
32. From the same abuser?
33. How often?
34. If the abuse was not from your parents, did your siblings ever tell your parents?
35. Did your siblings ever receive treatment for the abuse?
36. Were the abusers ever exposed to the authorities?
37. Did they ever receive judicial punishment?

HOMELESSNESS

This is a special kind of abuse, especially if you are a child that has experienced it. When you are homeless, you have long-term, maybe lifelong memory loss. If you survive, it will be a part of your soul for the rest of your life. It creates a permanent PTSD that will never go away. Trying to date or marry someone that has experienced this level of trauma is almost impossible. You will never understand their personal motivations or behaviors, and you may never be able to accept them. When those of us who have survived homelessness participate in a social function and are asked personal questions about our childhood, this subject will never be discussed. Not that we can't handle the topic, but the mentally healthy unfortunately cannot.

1. Have you ever been homeless?
2. How many times have you been homeless?
3. At what age was the first time you were homeless?
4. How long were you homeless?
5. How did you eat while homeless?
6. Where did you sleep?
7. Were you assaulted while homeless?
8. Were you sexually assaulted while homeless?
9. Did you ever receive psychological treatment for the homelessness?
10. Was it helpful?
11. Did your parent or parents ever abandon you?
12. Did you become homeless because of the abandonment?

13. How did you survive your homelessness event?
14. How has homelessness affected your life?
15. If it was your parents who abandoned you, how have you reconciled it with them?
16. Does your current family, like spouse or children, know you have been homeless?
17. Have you ever reconciled your homelessness with your siblings?
18. Have you ever run away from home?
19. What was the reason you ran away from home?
20. How many times have you run away?
21. How long were you gone from your home?
22. Did you eventually go back home?
23. Did the issue that caused you to run away get resolved once you went back home?
24. Were you homeless when you ran away?
25. How long have you been homeless?
26. Can you remember everything that happened to you while you were homeless, or do you have memory loss or gaps?

CRIMINAL ACTIVITY AND INCARCERATION

———

The mentally ill teach each other very young how to commit crimes. I knew a parole officer who told me he had entire families, from the grandfather to the grandson, on parole together. I landed in jail at ten years old.

1. Have you ever been incarcerated and at what age?
2. What were you incarcerated for?
3. How long were you incarcerated?
4. Have you ever been arrested?
5. How many times have you been arrested?
6. What were you arrested for?
7. When was the last time you were arrested?
8. Were any weapons used in the crimes you were arrested for?
9. Did anyone get hurt with the weapon you used during the crime?
10. Were you responsible for anyone getting hurt with the weapon that was used?
11. Do you currently have any outstanding warrants against you?
12. Have you ever gotten a parking ticket?
13. How many parking tickets have you gotten?
14. Have you paid all the fines off?
15. Were either of your parents ever incarcerated?
16. What were they incarcerated for?
17. How long did they serve in prison?

18. Did you ever visit them while they were in prison?
19. Were you or any of your siblings born during your parents' incarceration?
20. Were any of your grandparents ever incarcerated and for what?
21. For how long?
22. How many times have your grandparents been incarcerated?
23. Were any of your siblings or stepsiblings ever incarcerated?
24. For what offense?
25. For how long?
26. How many times?
27. Did you visit them during their incarceration?
28. How old were you when your siblings were incarcerated?
29. Have you ever stolen anything from the workplace?
30. Have you ever stolen anything from family members?
31. Have you ever destroyed any property that was not yours?
32. Have you ever embezzled any funds from an employer before?
33. How much did you steal from them?
34. Have you ever abused any animals, cats, dogs, other animals?
35. Have you ever killed an animal for any reason other than to feed you or your family?
36. Have you ever sexually abused anyone?
37. Who was it?
38. How many times have you sexually abused another person?
39. Have you ever bullied anyone?
40. What age did you bully that person?
41. How many times did you bully that person?
42. Did you physically or psychologically bully others?
43. How many times?
44. Have you ever financially abused anyone?
45. How many times have you financially abused someone before?
46. Did you make restitution to your victims?
47. How much did you have to pay back to your victims?

48. Have you ever physically assaulted anyone?
49. Was it someone close to you or a stranger?
50. How many times have you physically assaulted others?
51. Are you on any sexual registration systems with state or federal agencies?

FOSTER CARE AND ADOPTION

There are over four hundred thousand children in the United States living in foster care currently. Their family foundations are destroyed, either by drugs, alcohol, crime, abuse, or a thousand other reasons. One fact is certain, they were mostly born to the mentally ill. Their struggles are just beginning, and it will most likely take them a lifetime to rebuild their foundations, if they ever do.

1. Were you ever put into foster care?
2. At what age were you put in?
3. How long did you stay in foster care?
4. What was the reason that the state put you into foster care? Did your parent pass away? Was it because of drugs or alcohol? Was it sexual or physical abuse?
5. Did you age out while in foster care?
6. Where did you go when you aged out?
7. Did you become homeless?
8. Were any of your siblings put into foster care?
9. Were you able to stay with your siblings in the same family?
10. Did your foster care family or families treat you well?
11. Were any of them ever abusive to you?
12. If they abused you, what kind of abuse was it?
13. Were you ever adopted?
14. What age were you adopted?
15. Did the family that adopted you treat you well?
16. Were they ever abusive to you?

17. If they abused you, what kind of abuse was it?
18. Do you still associate with your foster care or adoptive family?
19. How often do you socialize with them?
20. What kinds of things do you do with them?
21. Did you have any foster care or adoptive siblings?
22. Do you still socialize with them?
23. How often do you socialize with them?
24. What kinds of things do you do with them socially?
25. If you and your natural-born siblings were put into foster care or adopted out and separated, have you ever reconnected with them?
26. What age were you when you reconnected?
27. How is your relationship now?
28. Do you ever talk with them or see them?
29. What kinds of social activities do you participate with them?
30. Do your siblings have children?
31. Have you ever met them?
32. Have you ever socialized with them?
33. Are you able to communicate with them about the separation?
34. Did you ever receive treatment for the issues associated with your separations from your siblings?

PSYCHIATRIC TREATMENT

———

This subject will be very sensitive but critical in your assessment while dating or planning to marry the mentally ill.

1. Have you ever been diagnosed with a psychiatric disorder?
2. When were you diagnosed?
3. Was the disorder considered genetic?
4. At what age did they diagnose you?
5. Have you ever been in therapy?
6. For how long?
7. Did you find it helpful?
8. Have you ever taken medications for a psychiatric disorder?
9. Are you currently taking medications?
10. Are you currently in therapy?
11. How long have you been in therapy?
12. Have you found it helpful?
13. Have you ever been hospitalized for a psychiatric issue?
14. How long was your stay?
15. How many times have you been hospitalized?
16. Have your parents or other family members ever received psychiatric treatments?
17. For how long?
18. Were they ever institutionalized?
19. Was your parents' disorder considered genetic?

RELATIONSHIP HISTORY

This topic can give you the knowledge you need to see what boundaries and behaviors your potential partner may have. As we age, this history can be critical to the information you need to acquire.

1. At what age did you start dating?
2. How many dates do you have a week, month, or year?
3. Have you ever had sex on your first date with someone?
4. How many dates do you have before you engage in sex?
5. How many one-night stands have you had?
6. Have you had multiple partners in your one-night stands?
7. In your one-night stands, have you had sex with same sex partners?
8. Have you ever had immediate casual sex?
9. How many times have you had immediate casual sex?
10. With an opposite sex partner or same sex partner?
11. How many long-term relationships have you had?
12. What has been their length?
13. Who broke the relationship or relationships off and why?
14. Was marriage ever talked about?
15. Have you ever been engaged?
16. How many times have you been engaged?
17. How many children do you have?
18. Are they from the same mother or father or are their more than one?
19. At what age was your first marriage?

20. Your second?
21. Your third?
22. Your fourth?
23. Have you ever been divorced?
24. How many times have you been divorced?
25. Do you still have a relationship with your exes and why?
26. Do you have stepchildren?
27. How many?
28. Do you still have a relationship with your stepchildren?
29. How often do you associate with your stepchildren?
30. What kinds of things do you do together?

JOB HISTORY

The mentally ill have a difficult time staying focused and committed to employers, especially if they are poor with no education. They have relationship issues with coworkers and employers because of their childhood abuses. Or they can be some of the hardest-working employees that the employer can ask for, especially ones who will work constantly with no personal breaks, and that may mean for years.

1. How many jobs have you had?
2. What kinds of jobs have you had?
3. How long do you usually spend at your job?
4. What is the longest time you have spent on a job?
5. Have you ever been terminated?
6. Why?
7. Have you ever received a promotion, award, or certificate of achievement?
8. How many hours a week do you usually work?
9. Do you ever take vacations?
10. Do you ever use up your sick leave or paid holidays?
11. What is the longest stretch of time that you have worked without a day off?
12. Month, six months, year, longer?
13. How many family functions a month, a year do you miss because of work?

FINANCES

———

Many reports site that finances are a major reason for divorce. Many couples do not even discuss finances while dating; it is one of those taboo subjects. Communicating about finances while dating and especially if the relationship is becoming serious is critical. Many families do not educate their children properly when it comes to finances; this leads to lack of knowledge and the possibility of making mistakes with your finances as a young adult. These mistakes can lead to major financial stress, but more important than that, it is time wasting and can lead to years of trying to recover from these mistakes. Finances can be a big indicator of paranoia in the family, from parents, siblings, and grandparents.

1. Do you have any debt?
2. How much debt do you carry?
3. How many credit cards do you have?
4. What are their limits?
5. Are they maxed out?
6. Have you ever been to a check-cashing location?
7. How many times?
8. Have you ever declared bankruptcy?
9. How many times?
10. What was the total dollar amount that you claimed on your bankruptcy?
11. What is your FICO score?
12. Do you own any life insurance policies?
13. Do you carry disability insurance on yourself?

14. Are you renting or buying?
15. Do you have any retirement funds set aside for things like 401(k)s or IRAs? What percentage of your check do you defer from your payroll, like 3 percent, 5 percent, 10 percent, or 15 percent?
16. Do you have health insurance for yourself?
17. If you have children, do you have health insurance on them?
18. Do you save money for your child's higher education, like college?
19. Do you have six months or one year of savings to replace your income if something like losing your job occurs?
20. Why not?
21. Do you have a will or trust?
22. Especially if you have children, why not?
23. Do you know if your parents have a will or trust?
24. If they have passed, did they have a will and trust?
25. If your grandparents have passed away, do you know if they had a will or trust?
26. If grandparents or parents have passed away, did they leave any financial resources for you and your siblings?
27. Did they leave any life insurance for you or your siblings?

SEXUAL HISTORY AND PREFERENCES

Sex in a relationship is extremely important for physical and psychological well-being. It can be one of the most joyful and loving actions couples participate in. The mentally ill may have been engaging in sex since they were young children. This can be a big part of the psychological trauma they have experienced in life. They may view sex completely different than you will. Knowing how their sexual history has shaped their current views, beliefs, and actions will help you communicate and understand their motivations better.

1. When did you have sex for the first time?
2. Was it with someone your own age or older?
3. Was it with someone of the opposite sex or same sex?
4. Do you choose to be monogamist?
5. Are you bisexual?
6. Do you enjoy having sex with one partner or multiple partners?
7. Do you enjoy oral sex?
8. Do you enjoy receiving and giving oral sex or both?
9. Do you have one-night stands?
10. Do you have a lot of one-night stands?
11. How often do you have one-night stands?
12. How many years have you participated in one-night stands?
13. Have you ever had a venereal disease?
14. What kind of disease have you had?
15. Is the disease still active and potentially permanent?

16. Do you enjoy anal sex?
17. Do you enjoy sex in public?
18. Do you enjoy pornography?
19. How often do you watch it?
20. Do you like watching it alone or with your sexual partner?
21. Do you enjoy using sex toys?
22. With your sexual partner or alone?
23. Do you ever participate in bondage?
24. Did you like it, and do you still participate?
25. Have you ever been diagnosed with a sexual addiction?
26. What was it for?
27. Have you ever received treatment for the addiction?
28. Is the addiction under control?
29. When was your last episode?
30. What is the longest time-period that you have had between dating partners?
31. What is the longest time-period that you have had between sexual encounters?
32. How long should you wait while dating before you become sexually active with your partner?
33. Have you ever had sex with a sibling?
34. Are you currently having sex with any of your siblings?
35. Are you currently having sex with other family members?
36. Have you ever paid for sex?
37. How many times?
38. What kind of sex do you participate in when you pay for it?
39. Do you have sex with the opposite sex or same-sex individuals when you pay for it?
40. Have you ever paid for sex while you were in a committed relationship?
41. Did you tell your partner about paying for sex?
42. Why not?
43. At what age did you pay for sex for the first time?
44. Who introduced you to paying for sex?
45. Was it a family member, friend, or did you just seek it out?

46. Would you pay for sex if you were in a committed relation-
    ship in the future?
47. Have you ever paid for sex and had your romantic partner
    participate with you?
48. Have any of your previous relationships ended because of
    sexual desires and activities?
49. Did the relationship end because you wanted something
    different from your partner?
50. Did the relationship end because of activities your partner
    wanted?

ALCOHOL

lcohol is one of the drugs of choice for the mentally ill; it's cheap, socially acceptable, and you can forget everything you did while using it if you drink enough. I believe it also allows you to suppress the memories that haunt your mind. It can push these memories down your entire life. Alcohol will be a constant drug of choice for the mentally ill; it will be invited everywhere they go and participate in almost everything they do. They usually were introduced to alcohol very early in life. As a young child, I grew up in bars, legal and illegal. According to the Center for Disease Control, Americans consume about thirty-five billion drinks per year. The FBI reports that DUI are the second-most common arrest made in the United States.

1. Do you drink alcohol?
2. At what age did you first start drinking?
3. How many times a week do you drink alcohol?
4. Do you drink alone or in a group?
5. How many drinks do you usually consume?
6. Have you ever blacked out from drinking?
7. Do you usually consume alcohol at family functions?
8. Sometimes, almost always?
9. Does your family consume alcohol?
10. Do they consume alcohol at family functions?
11. Sometimes, almost always?
12. Do you consume alcohol at social events, like sporting events or parties?

13. Who first introduced you to alcohol?
14. Have you ever driven a car after or while you were drinking?
15. Have you ever had a DUI?
16. How many have you had?
17. Have your driving privileges ever had to be modified because of your drinking?
18. Have you ever had your driver's license revoked or suspended?
19. Have you ever driven a vehicle while intoxicated with your children in the car?
20. Have you ever drunk alcohol around your children?
21. How often do you drink alcohol around your children, daily, weekly, monthly, just on social events?
22. Have you encouraged your minor children to drink alcohol?
23. How many times?
24. Did they get drunk?
25. At what age did you first introduce them to drinking alcohol?
26. Have you ever wrecked your care while driving?
27. Have you ever drunk alcohol while pregnant?
28. Has anyone in your family ever died from alcoholism or alcohol-related illnesses?
29. Have you ever had to admit yourself to an alcohol rehab facility?
30. For how long?
31. How many times?
32. Have any family members ever been admitted to a rehab facility?
33. For how long?
34. How many times?

DRUG USAGE

Drug use is another product of choice that the mentally ill use to suppress the pain and trauma they are trying to survive from. According to Addictionhelp.com, as of 2020, over thirty-seven million people twelve and older have used drugs in the past thirty days. The FBI reports that drug arrests are the number one arrest they make.

1. Do you use any drugs, like marijuana, cocaine, meth, barbiturates, pain medications, heroin, for recreational usage?
2. How often a week, month, or year do you use them?
3. Have you ever driven a motor vehicle, like car, motorboat, motorcycle, or RV, while using drugs?
4. How many times have you used drugs while driving a motor vehicle?
5. Have you ever been arrested while driving under the influence of drugs?
6. How many times?
7. Have you ever been admitted to a rehab facility for drug usage?
8. How many times?
9. For how long?
10. When was the last time you entered a facility?
11. Have you ever done drugs around your children?
12. How often do you do drugs around your children?
13. At what age did you first introduce drugs to your children?
14. Have you ever done drugs with your children?

15. How often do you do drugs with your children?
16. At what age did you first do drugs with your children?
17. Have you ever overdosed?
18. How many times?
19. Have you ever died and been revived?
20. Have you ever done drugs while pregnant?
21. How often?
22. How many times?
23. Did the baby have any neurological disorders because of the exposure?
24. What has been the long-term effects to the child?
25. Has any family member ever died from an overdose?
26. Has any member of your family ever had to enter a drug rehabilitation program?
27. Who first introduced you to drugs?
28. How old were you when you first used drugs?
29. How many years have you been using drugs?
30. How much do you spend on drugs monthly or annually?
31. Have you ever made drugs?
32. Have you ever sold drugs?
33. When was the last time you sold drugs?

HUNTING, FISHING, AND WEAPON OWNERSHIP AND USAGE

Hunting, fishing, and gun ownership are part of the American fabric. But when it comes to the mentally ill, it can be signs of troubling behavior and uncontrollable paranoia. It is estimated that Americans own over four hundred million weapons. That is what they consider registered; how many are owned illegally?

1. Do you hunt for sport, pleasure, or sustenance?
2. How many times a year do you hunt?
3. What kind of animals do you hunt for?
4. Do you hunt alone or with a group?
5. Do you consume alcohol when you hunt?
6. Do you use any drugs while hunting?
7. Do you taxidermy any of your kills?
8. How many weapons do you own?
9. What kinds of weapons do you own?
10. How much do you spend annually on weapons and ammunition?
11. Do you carry a weapon on your person?
12. Have you ever pulled your weapon on another human?
13. For what reason?
14. Have you taught your children how to use the weapons?
15. Do you take them hunting for sport, recreation, or sustenance?
16. Have you ever pulled a weapon on any person in front of your children?

SEXUAL OCCUPATIONS

Because of the sexual history of the mentally ill, especially if they began as children having sex with adults, their boundaries and lifestyle choices may not be socially traditional. Or they may have no psychological reasonings and just really enjoy sex.

1. Have you ever been a sex worker?
2. What kind of sex worker?
3. How long did you do that job?
4. Have you ever been a stripper?
5. Partially or fully unclothed?
6. For how long?
7. Have you ever performed in an adult movie?
8. What kind of movie?
9. How long were you in the industry?
10. How many productions were you in?
11. Does your family know that you have been in adult movies?
12. Do they approve or disapprove?
13. Have you ever performed sex acts for a webcam?
14. Have you ever been arrested for being a sex worker?
15. Would you ever want to be a sex worker again?
16. If you have children, do they know you have been a sex worker?
17. If so, how do they feel about it?
18. Have you ever been romantically involved while you were a sex worker?
19. Was your partner in the industry also?
20. Would you pursue a romantic relationship in the future if you are still a sex worker?

ABUSE TOWARD A SPOUSE OR CHILD

The mentally ill may have grown up in an abusive family and experienced the traumas of physical and psychological abuse. As adults, they may be abusing their loved ones currently or in their past. You must know before it is too late for you to get out of the relationship.

1. Have you ever had a physical confrontation with a romantic partner?
2. Did you slap them, punch them, or kick them?
3. Have you ever thrown anything at your partner before?
4. How many times were you physical with them?
5. Did they ever need medical treatment because of your physical abuse?
6. Did the physical activity lead to you breaking up?
7. Have you ever had a physical confrontation with your partner in front of your child?
8. Have you ever physically abused your child?
9. How many times have you physically abused your child?
10. Did they ever have to receive medical treatment because of your abuse?
11. How many times has your child received medical treatment because of your abuse?
12. What kinds of physical abuse have you done to your child or children?
13. Were the authorities ever called in to protect the child from you?

14. How many times were the authorities called in?
15. Were you ever incarcerated because of the abuse of your child?
16. How many times have you been incarcerated because of the abuse of your child?
17. Has any of your exes ever physically abused your child or children?
18. What kind of abuse did they perpetrate against your child?
19. Were authorities ever called against any of your exes for abusing your children?
20. Were your children ever put into protective custody because of your abuse of them?
21. Were they ever put into protective custody because of the abuse they received from an ex?
22. Have you ever been arrested because of abuse of a romantic partner?
23. How many times?
24. Have you ever served a prison sentence because of your abuse of a romantic partner?
25. How many times?
26. For how long?

RELATIONSHIP TO THEIR CHILDREN

The dynamic of how the mentally ill interact with their children is very important, especially as their children age. You will see very strained relationships, communication problems, and lost opportunities on both sides for a loving and caring relationship. As children age, the damage to the relationship is obvious.

1. How often do you talk with your children?
2. What kind of activities do you participate with them?
3. When is the last time you participated with them?
4. If you have grandchildren, when is the last time you have seen them?
5. Do you ever do anything with them by themselves, or is everything coordinated through a family event, like Christmas?
6. Do you babysit the grandchildren?
7. How often?
8. Do you have a good relationship with your child's spouse and in-laws?
9. Have you ever had a separate activity with your in-laws that did not include your children or grandchildren?
10. Why not?
11. Do you allow any of your children around convicted felons?
12. Do your exes allow your children around any convicted felons, especially sex offenders?
13. Do you ever go on vacations with your children or grandchildren?

14. Where is the last place you went to?
15. How long ago was that?
16. Do you have any plans in your estate to leave funds for your grandchildren's education or first home purchase?

SCHOOL ACTIVITIES

Mentally ill parents and grandparents are not interested in their children's or grandchildren's activities or are so involved in their own psychological tornadoes that they are usually absentee when it comes to school activities. Or the family is so disconnected they are never socializing together in these activities.

1. What kind of school activities did you participate in?
2. Did you participate throughout your schooltime, or did you stop at any time?
3. Did your parents, grandparents, or siblings ever participate in your activities?
4. How often did they attend?
5. Whenever you qualified for an activity, did your parents ever refuse to pay the cost of that participation especially if they could afford it?
6. Did your parents support your educational goals for a higher education?
7. Did your grandparents and siblings support your goals?
8. If your grandparents passed away while you were in school, did they leave any funds for your educational efforts?
9. While your grandparents were alive, did they provide any financial support for your higher educational efforts especially if they could afford it?

10. Did your parents help you plan and implement your goals and objectives for a higher education, or were you left to figure it out on your own?
11. What level of education do you have, drop out, high school degree, technical school, a certification of some kind, some college, full college, university degree, PhD?
12. Do you still associate with your high school friends or college friends?
13. How often do you associate with them and what kinds of activities do you participate with them in?

SUICIDE ATTEMPTS

Suicide attempts are a major red flag of severe psychological distress. You must know the history of your potential romantic partners' attempts or their family members' attempts before you can ever conceive having a long-term relationship with them. This is one of those big secrets that can make or break your commitment to the relationship.

1. Have you ever attempted suicide?
2. What age were you when you attempted suicide?
3. How many times?
4. How did you attempt it?
5. Did you receive psychiatric treatment for the attempt?
6. Are you currently taking any medications because of your suicide attempt?
7. Has any of your parents attempted suicide?
8. How many times?
9. Did they die of suicide?
10. Have any of your siblings ever attempted suicide?
11. How many times?
12. Did they pass away because of it?
13. Did any of your grandparents ever attempt suicide?
14. How many times?
15. Did any of them pass away because of suicide?
16. Has any of your children ever attempted suicide?
17. How did they attempt it?
18. If any suicide attempts were committed by family members, did they receive psychiatric treatment?

RELATIONSHIP TO EXES CURRENTLY

W hen you begin the dating process, knowing as much about the relationship between the mentally ill and their exes is very important, especially if children are involved. The psychological issues of the exes must play a role in your assessment when deciding to date or marry. The ex's current and past psychological issues should be a factor for you to consider, especially if you have children with your new partner and your children will be involved with these exes.

1. Do you and your ex get along currently?
2. Why did you separate or divorce?
3. If you had children, what ex is that with?
4. Have you ever had sex with your ex once you divorced?
5. How many times?
6. Are you currently having sex with them?
7. How often?
8. Has that ex remarried?
9. How many times?
10. Did that ex have more children and how many?
11. Do you have a good relationship with your ex's current partners?
12. If you do not, why?
13. Are you comfortable having your children around the new ex's partner?
14. And if not, why?
15. Do you know the history of your ex's new partner?

16. Their family history?
17. What is their status with their families? How do you participate with them?
18. Have your exes ever received mental health treatments?
19. How many times and for what?
20. Do your exes take any medications for mental health issues?
21. What is the family history of your exes?
22. Do they participate with their families socially?
23. Do they take your children around their families?
24. And if not, why not?
25. Have your exes ever been abusive, sexually, physically, psychologically, or financially, to your children?
26. How often did they abuse your children?
27. Did your children ever receive psychological help for the abuse?
28. Were authorities ever called in because of the abuse they received from your exes?
29. Was any criminal chargers or actions ever taken against your exes for the abuse your children received from them?
30. Did any of your exes' romantic partners or spouses ever abuse your ex?
31. Did any of your exes' romantic partners or spouses ever abuse your children?
32. Did they abuse them sexually, physically, or psychologically?
33. How many times did they abuse your children?
34. Were authorities ever called because of the abuse of your child?
35. Do you still allow your children to be associated with your ex's partner?
36. Are any of your exes on sex registries?
37. Are any of your exes ex-spouses or current romantic partners on any sex registries?
38. Have your exes ever been incarcerated?
39. How many times?
40. For what?
41. For how long?

42. Has any of your exes' ex or current romantic partners ever been incarcerated?
43. How many times?
44. For what?
45. For how long?
46. Are they still incarcerated?

SMOKING TOBACCO USAGE

Medical experts have known for decades how damaging tobacco can be to humans. The mentally ill will ignore all the evidence and advertising that is given daily and still engage in this very self-defeating behavior. Deciding to date someone who smokes or chews tobacco may not even be a discussion to have, but remember, they may hide their current or past usage. I started smoking when I was about five. Most people I know have no idea I ever smoked, and they never ask.

1. Have you ever smoked?
2. When did you begin?
3. Do you smoke currently?
4. What kinds of tobacco do you use, just smoking tobacco or chewing?
5. Do you smoke daily, weekly, monthly, or just on special occasions?
6. Do you smoke in front of your children?
7. Have you ever allowed your children to smoke with you?
8. Have you ever smoked while pregnant?
9. Who first introduced you to smoking?
10. Your parents?
11. Your siblings?
12. Other family members?
13. Or someone else?
14. Did any of your family members ever die from smoking or using tobacco products?

15. Do you vape?
16. When did you first start?
17. How often do you vape, daily, weekly, monthly, or just whenever?
18. Do you vape with any family members?
19. When is the first time you vaped with them?
20. Who first introduced you to vaping?
21. Have you ever vaped while pregnant?
22. How often, daily, weekly, monthly, or just whenever?

NEGLECT AS A CHILD

Neglect comes in so many forms; it can be neglect of time, medical needs, education, nutrition, financial support, abandonment, physical activities, psychological treatments, and social functioning. Mentally ill parents do not have the psychological ability to have compassion for their children. They are so involved with their psychological issues they have no concern for what their child is experiencing or what needs their child have. Poverty can exacerbate all these issues for children.

1. Did your parents ever leave you alone for an extended time-period?
2. Like a day, days, week, month or longer?
3. When your parent left, did they provide oversight from a relative, neighbor, or sitter?
4. Or were you just left alone to take care of yourself?
5. Did your parent provide food for you to eat while they were gone?
6. Or did you have to care for yourself any way you could?
7. Did your parent leave money for you to use for food?
8. How many days did you go without food?
9. Did your parent ever leave information on how to contact them?
10. Were you supported by your parents in daily and weekly school assignments?

11. Did your parents ever provide medical treatments for things like dentists, optometrists, or annual checkups from pediatricians?
12. If you got sick with a cold or other ailment, did your parents provide you treatments?
13. If you were sexually abused from someone other than your parents, did your parents ever know about the sexual abuse?
14. Did you ever feel safe and protected from your parents?
15. Did you ever feel like you were nothing to your parents?
16. Do you think your parents really did not care if you lived or died?
17. Do you think anyone in your family, grandparents, siblings, other family members, ever really cared if you lived or died?
18. When you experienced traumatic events in your childhood, did your parents ever get you psychological help?
19. Were you ever abandoned by your parent or parents?
20. How many times were you abandoned by your parent or parents?
21. Did anyone in your family ever come to look for you while you were abandoned?
22. How did the behavior of your parents, siblings, grandparents, other family members make you feel about having children of your own?
23. Do you think you ever want to have children?
24. Why not?
25. What would ever change your thinking about having your own children?
26. If you had children, would anyone in your family ever care if they lived or died?
27. If you had children, could you ever count on any family member to take care of your child and provide for their needs?

PSYCHOLOGICAL EDUCATION AND SELF-ASSESSMENT ANALYSIS

When the mentally ill begin to come out of the fog of their childhoods, they may begin to seek professional assistance from a psychological professional or begin to self-educate themselves or do both. I think this will depend on their personal finances more than anything. If they are poor, they will have to self-educate, and that is perfectly alright. Remember, I do not believe any chaos chaser will ever seek this kind of information to heal themselves. I think one of the biggest reasons people do not attempt to educate themselves about psychology is narcissism, the belief in their own superiority of not needing this kind of knowledge.

1. Have you ever read any books on psychiatry or psychology?
2. What did you find helpful from them?
3. Have you ever read any self-help books?
4. How many?
5. Did you find them helpful?
6. Have you read any relationship-improvement books?
7. How many? Did you find them helpful?
8. Have you ever taken the ACE (Adverse Childhood Experiences) test?
9. Have you ever read anything about CPTSD (complex post-traumatic stress disorder)?
10. Have you ever read the DSM-5 (*Diagnostic Statistical Manual of Mental Disorder*)? It is the diagnostic manual

that the mental health community uses for understanding their patients' needs and how to treat them.
11. Do you do any activities that are considered self-healing?
12. Meditation, yoga, exercising, special diets? Vitamin regimen?
13. Do you own any books on psychiatry or psychology?
14. If you have children, have you ever introduced them to the knowledge of psychiatry or psychology?
15. Do your parents and siblings ever talk to you about the treatments they may be receiving?
16. Do your parents or siblings ever talk about psychiatric or psychological text they have read or are reading?

AGING PARENTS OR FAMILY
MEMBERS WITH MEDICAL NEEDS

The mentally ill's relationship with their aging parents or family members who have medical needs will be enlightening to you. You will be able to see the result of the arc of their relationship. How they participate with their family members will clearly expose the compassion or lack thereof when it comes to their feelings to their aging parent or a family member that has serious medical needs.

1. Have you ever provided care for an aging parent or grandparent in their home or a facility?
2. How long did the care last?
3. Did you or your siblings take the aging parent into your home for care?
4. For how long?
5. What kind of care did your loved one need, home care, assisted living, or long-term care?
6. Were you the main caretaker or did your siblings participate?
7. Did any other family members participate?
8. How often did siblings and other family members participate in the care?
9. How was the cost of care paid for?
10. Did you and your siblings agree when it came to finances?
11. Why not?
12. Did your siblings not participate with your parent's care because of something that was wrong in their relationship?

13. Or were your siblings just not concerned?
14. Have you or do you have a family member that has serious medical needs?
15. Do you participate in their care?
16. How often do you participate in their care?
17. How do you participate in their care?
18. Do you ever visit with them?
19. When is the last time you visited with them?
20. What did you do with them?
21. Do you ever take them a meal?
22. Do you ever call them to comfort them?
23. How often do you call them?
24. When is the last time that you called them?
25. If your family member was terminally ill, did you participate in their final days either at home or in hospice?
26. How long did you participate in their care?
27. What did you do for them during their final days?
28. Did any of your siblings or other family members participate with your loved ones during their final days?
29. Did you participate as a family or individually?
30. If your loved one was in their final moments, were you responsible for making the final decision to remove life-support systems?
31. If your loved one was in their final moments, did your family participate in their removal of life-support systems?

FINAL ARRANGEMENTS

T he mentally ill will abandon each other right to the bitter end. How they deal with the death of a family member will show you how they might deal with you when your arrangements must be made.

1. Has any of your parents or grandparents passed away?
2. Were you the primary facilitator of the funeral arrangements, or did other family members like siblings or parents assist you?
3. Did you go to the funeral home alone, or did other family members go with you?
4. Did the family member who passed preplan any arrangements, or were they left to the family to make?
5. Did they choose direct cremation or traditional burial?
6. Was there any headstone placed?
7. Do you ever visit the grave or marker of your loved one?
8. Do you and your siblings ever visit together?
9. How often?
10. When was the last time you visited together?
11. Do you have any cemetery arrangements around your loved ones?
12. Are you planning in the future to purchase space around your loved ones?
13. Have you ever talked to your children about your funeral and cemetery arrangements?
14. Why not?

15. Have you made your funeral arrangements and paid for them?

16. Have you left any instructions for your final arrangements and set aside funds for the cost?

SOCIAL AND RELIGIOUS ACTIVITIES

Social and religious activities can show you very quickly what level of commitment they have to a function or group. Do they participate in these activities alone or with family members? How obsessed are they about these activities, and can this level of commitment fit into your life plans with a potential partner? You can also see how involved they are with their families in these activities and how they might treat each other because of their beliefs. It will also show you their beliefs about you if you're not a religious person.

1. Do you participate in any social activities?
2. How often?
3. How long have you been participating in these activities?
4. What do you enjoy about them?
5. Are there any social activities that you would like to pursue in the future?
6. What is intriguing about your choice?
7. How often do you participate in these activities, daily, weekly, randomly?
8. Do you participate with any of your siblings in these social activities?
9. Do you participate with your parents in these social activities?
10. Do you participate with any of your aunts, uncles, cousins in any of these social activities?

11. When was the last time you participated with your family in these activities?
12. How many times a year do you participate together?
13. Why don't you participate with your families in these activities?
14. Do you belong to any religious organizations?
15. How long have you been attending them?
16. How often do you attend, daily, weekly, monthly, or only on special occasions?
17. Do you currently participate in any religious activities with your siblings, parents, aunts, uncles, cousins?
18. Did you ever participate with your family members in religious activities?
19. Did you participate with your family when you were a child, young adult, or adult?
20. Have you ever been disowned by your family because of their religious beliefs?
21. Does your family think you are not going to be joining them in heaven because of what activity or belief that got you disowned?
22. Have you ever disowned any family member because of your religious beliefs?
23. Do you still have a relationship with that disowned family member?
24. Do you ever socialize with them?
25. What kinds of things do you do with them?
26. Are there any actions that your children could commit that would demand that you disown them?
27. Do you believe that the family members you have disowned are going to be joining you in heaven?
28. Do you socialize with any nonreligious individuals?
29. What do you do together?
30. How often do you socialize with them?
31. Do you socialize with their families?
32. How often do you socialize with their families?
33. What activities do you participate in with them?

34. How many nonreligious people would you consider a close friend?
35. How long have you been friends?
36. Have you ever dated a nonreligious person?
37. How long did you date them?
38. Would you ever consider creating a permanent relationship or marrying a person who didn't believe in your chosen religion?
39. Why did your relationship with a nonreligious person not continue?
40. While dating a nonreligious individual, did you ever think they would not be allowed to join you in the afterlife?
41. Have you ever dated someone of another faith?
42. How long did you date for?
43. Have any of your parents or siblings been a religious leader?
44. How long were they in a leadership role?
45. Did they retire from their leadership role?
46. Were they ever dismissed from their leadership duties?
47. What was the reasoning for their dismissal?
48. Did you ever attend a religious school?
49. Did you graduate?
50. Have you ever been a religious leader?
51. How long were you a religious leader?
52. What made you stop being a religious leader?
53. Have your ever been fired as a religious leader?
54. What was it for?
55. Have you ever been expelled from a religious group?
56. What was the reasoning?
57. Have you ever been involved in a cult?
58. How long were you involved?
59. How did you get yourself out?
60. Have you received any psychological treatment because of your cult activities?
61. Has any of your family been involved in a cult?
62. Have any of your children been involved in a cult?
63. What did you like most about the cult?

64. What did you like the least?
65. Could you see yourself ever being involved in a cult again?
66. Do you participate in any charitable activities?
67. How often do you participate?
68. Do you donate to any charitable organizations?
69. When was the last time you donated to a charitable organization?

SPORT ACTIVITIES

Sporting activities are good for the soul and enjoyable individually, socially, and with your family. It can also be very negative if the person you want to create a relationship has a gambling problem or is a gambling addict. According to Wallethub.com, US consumers experience over $100 billion per year in total gambling losses annually. Who knows what the number is illegally.

1. What's your favorite sporting activity?
2. Do you play or watch?
3. Do you gamble on sporting events?
4. How often do you place bets?
5. How much do you usually bet on a given event?
6. What is the most money you have ever bet on an event?
7. What is the greatest amount of money that you have won at an event?
8. What is the most amount of money that you have lost on an event?
9. Do you like to gamble alone?
10. Or do you like to gamble with others?
11. Who first introduced you to gambling?
12. When was the first time you gambled?
13. Have you ever lost money gambling that was supposed to be used for household expenses?
14. Did the lost money cause harm to anyone you love?
15. How many times have you lost money that was supposed to be used for household expenses?

16. Do you drink while gambling?
17. Do you do drugs while gambling?
18. Do you get angry when you lose your money?
19. Have you ever gotten into a physical altercation during a gambling event with someone else?
20. Did you or they get injured?
21. Was it a severe injury?
22. Did either one of you require medical treatment?
23. How many altercations have you had over gambling?
24. Have you had these altercations in public events or private events?
25. Has your gambling ever caused you to lose a personal romantic relationship?
26. How many times have you lost romantic relationships over gambling?
27. How long did these relationships last before you lost them?
28. If you have children, have you ever gambled around them?
29. Have you ever shown them how to gamble?
30. Were you drinking or doing drugs when you gambled around your children?

POLITICAL BELIEFS AND ACTIVITIES

In 2023, America has seen the most chaotic activity in the history of our country when it comes to our political processes. Nothing has been more apparent and obvious as to the proof of induced psychosis than our politic beliefs and activities over the past few years. I did not include political beliefs and activities in the original draft of this book, but with where we are today, I could not ignore it, and I had to include it. With the tribal divisions that are prevalent in our political bodies, it is critical that this become a category of questions when you are dating and thinking of marrying someone with psychological issues. Their inducement from political leaders is crucial in your decision to date or potentially marrying them. Individuals with induced psychosis may not have been taught their political beliefs from their parents, but it doesn't mean that as adults, they cannot be psychologically manipulated by political leadership. If you do not agree with each other's political beliefs in today's climate, a romantic relationship may not be possible.

1. Have you or would you ever vote for any political leader who has been indicted for conspiracy against America?
2. Have you or would you ever vote for any political leader who has kidnapped children from their parents?
3. Have you or would you ever vote for any political leader who has withheld approved funding for military use to an American-allied country?
4. Have you or would you ever vote for a political leader who has told verifiable falsehoods to the American people?

5. Have you or would you ever vote for a political leader who has been accused and sued for rape?
6. Have you or would you ever vote for a political leader who chose to side with a murderous dictator over Americas intelligence agencies and law enforcement agencies?
7. Have you ever voted for or would you vote for any political leader who has attempted to overturn a valid election?
8. Have you or would you ever vote for any political leader who has lost multiple lawsuits trying to overthrow the voting will of the people?
9. Would you ever vote for any political leader who has or would threaten any poll workers or political employees?
10. Would you or have you ever voted for a political leader who makes public threats against prosecutors and their family members?
11. Would you or have you ever voted for any political leader who during a national crisis, like a pandemic, would withhold medical equipment and services?
12. Would you or have you ever voted for any political leader who during a national crisis, like a pandemic, misdirect the medical advice from legitimate medical specialists and their information to help them politically?
13. Have you or would you ever vote for a political leader who has been impeached?
14. Have you or would you ever vote for a political leader who has been indicted and or convicted of espionage?
15. How long have you been affiliated with the political party you have chosen currently?
16. How many times have you voted the party line in past elections?
17. Have you or do you volunteer for any campaigns?
18. How many times a year do you volunteer?
19. What political party do you donate funds to?
20. How much do you donate?
21. Do you donate weekly, monthly, or annually?

22. Do you listen to any radio or television stations that spread falsehoods?
23. Do you listen to any radio stations or watch any television channels that have future lawsuits against them for spreading falsehoods?
24. Do you listen to any radio stations or watch any television channels that have been sued for falsehoods and had to make a cash settlement to end the lawsuit?
25. Would you listen to any radio station or watch any television channel that has current lawsuits against them for their falsehoods?
26. Does your family follow the same political party as you?
27. If your family does not follow the same party as you, how has that affected your relationship with them?
28. Are you still communicating with your family currently about political topics?
29. Have you ever had a romantic relationship breakup because of political disagreements?
30. Was it because of your affiliations or your partners?
31. Did your parents or another family member get you involved politically?
32. When did they first introduce you to the political experience?
33. Have you ever marched for a political event?
34. How often?
35. When is the last time you marched and for what event?
36. What newspapers do you read?
37. What podcasts do you listen to?
38. Do you listen daily, weekly, less?
39. What radio stations do you listen to?
40. Do you listen daily, weekly, less?
41. What television stations do you get your politics from?
42. Do you watch daily, weekly, less?

I hope these questions help you in making your assessment during your dating stage. I wish you all the best.

Here is a list of some of the books I have read on my journey to educate myself in the world of psychology and self-analysis. I hope they will help you as much as they've helped me. Take care.

Psychological reading

- *The Complex PTSD Workbook* by Arielle Schwartz, PhD, Althea Press 2016
- *DSM-5* (*Diagnostic and Statistical Manual of Mental Disorders* fifth edition) by American Psychiatric Association, 2013
- *The Psychopath Test* by Jon Ronson Riverhead Books, 2011
- *Madness In Civilization* by Andrew Scull, Princeton University Press Princeton and Oxford
- *Too Much and Never Enough* by Mary L. Trump, PhD, Simon and Schuster
- *Madness: A Brief History* by Roy Porter, Oxford University Press
- *Psychological Testing and Assessment* tenth edition by Ronald Jay Cohen, W. Joel Schneider, and Renee M. Tobin McGraw Hill

ABOUT THE AUTHOR

Edward Rieger was born in Kansas City, Missouri, in 1960. He grew up as one of nine children to a single parent who struggled with alcoholism. He has sixty-three years of direct knowledge and experience of how mental illness is ingrained in children from their mentally ill parents. He shares, like never before, how the mentally ill's upbringing is one of the biggest factors in trying to figure out why they think and behave the way they do. His experiences will shed a new way of evaluating the psychological makeup of the person you are trying to create a possible lifelong relationship with.